Fats
for a Healthy Body

Jillian Powell

Heinemann Library
Chicago, Illinois

Printed and bound in China by CTPS

13 12 11 10 09
10 9 8 7 6 5 4 3 2 1

Library of Congress Cataloging-in-Publication Data
Powell; Jillian.
    Fats for a healthy body / Jillian Powell.
       p. cm. -- (Body needs)
    Summary: Discusses what fats are, how they are absorbed   and stored in the body, how the body uses fats, and health problems caused by fats.
    Includes bibliographical references and index.
    ISBN 978 1 432921 87 3 (hb)
    ISBN 978 1 432921 93 4 (pb)
    1. Fatty acids in human nutrition--Juvenile literature.
2. Lipids in human nutrition--Juvenile literature. [1. Fat.
2 Nutrition.]
    I. Title. II. Series.
    QP751.P695 2003
    612.3'97--dc21

                                        2002012643

Acknowledgments
We would like to thank the following for permission to reproduce photographs: ©Corbis: pp. **16**, **36**, **37** (Bohemian Nomad Picture Makers), **39** (Stock market/ Ariel Skelley), **41** (Macduff Everton), **43**; ©Gareth Boden: pp. **7**, **32**; ©Getty Stone: pp. **29**, **33**; ©Liz Eddison: pp. **9**, **21**, **22**, **27**, **38**; ©Photodisc: pp. **25**, **28**; ©Photolibrary Group Ltd: pp. **4** (Foodpix/Gentl & Hyers), **5** (Pacific Stock/Erik Aeder), **19** (Aflo Sports/Aflo Foto Agency) **31** (Corbis); ©SPL: pp. **13** (Chris Priest and Mark Clarke), **14**, **26** (Will and Deni McIntyre), **35**; ©Trevor Clifford: p. **24**; ©USDA Center for Nutrition Policy and Promotion p. **42**.

Cover photograph of olive oil, black olives and olive branch in bowl, reproduced with permission of PhotoLibrary Group/Food Collection.

We would like to thank Dr. Sarah Schenker and Nicole A. Clark for their invaluable assistance in the preparation of this book.

Contents

Any words appearing in the text in bold, **like this**, are explained in the glossary.

Why Do We Need to Eat?

Most people eat two or three main meals a day. We eat because we get hungry and because we enjoy the taste of food. At the same time we satisfy one of the body's essential needs—we supply it with all the chemicals it needs to stay alive and healthy.

Cells

Your body is made up of millions of tiny **cells**. For example, your bones consist of bone cells and your skin of skin cells. Most cells are so small you need a microscope to see them, but each one is working hard to carry out a particular task. To do this, your cells need a continual supply of **energy**. They also need many different chemicals, which come mainly from your food. These chemicals are called **nutrients**.

Nutrients

Carbohydrates, fats, **proteins**, **vitamins**, and **minerals** are all different types of nutrients. Most foods contain a lot of one type of nutrient, but they contain small amounts of other nutrients, too. Together, nutrients provide energy and materials that the body needs to work properly and to grow. This book is about fats—what they are and how the body uses them. However, since fats work alongside other nutrients, we will first take a look at the part they play to make you healthy.

Whether you eat your food at home, at school, or in a restaurant, you should try to eat a balanced and nutritious meal.

Energy food

Your body's main need is for food that provides energy. Everything you do uses energy—not just running and moving around, but also thinking, eating, keeping warm, and even sleeping. Carbohydrates and fats provide energy. The body burns carbohydrates, just like a car engine burns gasoline, and it needs a big supply every day. Foods such as bread, pasta, potatoes, and sugar are mainly carbohydrates and are your body's main source of energy. Fats are found in foods such as oils, margarines, and butters, and they have the highest **calorie** content when compared to carbohydrates and protein.

Protein

Protein is needed to make new cells and repair any damaged ones. Protein is the main substance found in muscles, skin, and internal **organs**. Your body is constantly renewing the cells that make up your skin, muscles, and all other parts of your body. Cells consist mainly of water and protein, so to build new cells your body uses proteins that you get from foods such as meat, fish, eggs, beans, and cheese. It is particularly important that children take in plenty of protein, because they are still growing and their bodies need it to make millions of extra cells.

When you do sporting activities, your body uses the energy that you get from your food.

What Are Fats?

It is the food we eat that helps our bodies grow, stay healthy, and have energy. For a balanced diet, we need to eat a range of foods from three main food types: carbohydrates, proteins, and fats.

Energy stores

We eat fats in lots of different foods. We eat animal fats in meat and dairy foods, such as butter, milk, and cream. We eat vegetable oils in nuts and seeds, and as liquid oils such as sunflower and olive oil for frying foods or dressing salads. Fats are also used in cooked or processed foods, such as cakes, cookies, chips, French fries, and pastries.

Do you need fats?

Fats have a bad reputation because they are high in calories (or **kilojoules**), so they can be fattening. If you eat too many fried, fatty foods, you will increase your risk of becoming overweight, or **obese**. But not all fats are bad for you. You need some fats in your diet to keep your body healthy.

You need fats in your diet to give you energy and help you grow. Having fats in the diet also helps your body absorb vitamins A, D, E, and K. Fat stored in the body helps keep you warm and cushions and protects organs like your **liver** and kidneys.

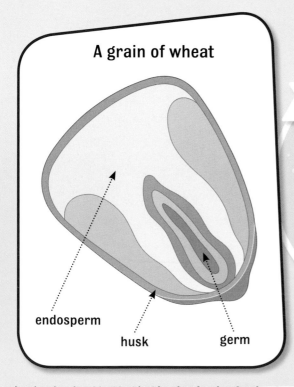

A grain of wheat

endosperm

husk

germ

CORN OIL

The oil in a seed of corn comes from inside the **germ**. If you cut a popcorn kernel in half, you can see the **husk**, **starch**, and germ. The oil can be pressed out of the germ. It takes the grain from 15 ears of corn to make 15 milliliters (0.5 ounces) of corn oil.

Fatty acids

Some foods contain **fatty acids** that your body needs to stay healthy. Your body cannot make these fatty acids. You can only get them from fats that you eat. You need them to keep your brain and nerve cells healthy. They make skin oils and help form chemicals called **hormones** that you need for many body processes. They also help your body fight off germs and diseases and repair damaged **tissue**.

Fats also make food taste better and improve its texture. Cakes, doughnuts, and cookies are tasty to eat.

 Fat fact

Foods like bacon, burgers, and fries are tempting to eat because fats add flavor and texture to food. This is what food scientists call "mouth feel."

 Foods that contain fats give you lots of energy.

What Is in Fats?

All the fats and oils in foods that we eat are made out of fatty acids. There are many different types of fatty acid, but they are all made from the same chemicals. A fatty acid is a chain of **carbon atoms**, with **oxygen** atoms attached on one end and **hydrogen** atoms attached on the other end.

Foods that contain fats and foods that contain carbohydrates both provide energy when we eat them. But fats are a richer source of energy than carbohydrates. Each gram of fat carries 9 calories of energy—more than twice as many as a gram of carbohydrate does.

Fatty acids

There are over 40 different types of fatty acids in foods and about 21 in the average diet. There are three main types of fatty acids: **saturated**, **polyunsaturated**, and **monounsaturated** fatty acids. Scientists tell the different types apart by counting how many hydrogen atoms they have.

A **molecule** of saturated fatty acid has the maximum possible number of hydrogen atoms attached to every carbon atom. Scientists say it is "saturated" with hydrogen because it cannot take any more. This type of fatty acid is mainly found in animal foods like meat and cream.

Some fatty acids are missing one pair of hydrogen atoms in the middle of the molecule. There is one gap or "unsaturation," so they are called monounsaturated fatty acids. ("Mono" means "one.") They are found in foods like olive oil and peanuts.

Fat fish fact

Tuna and salmon are cold-water fish. They are high in polyunsaturated fats. If these fish were high in saturated fat, which is solid in cold temperatures, they would freeze solid in icy water!

FIND THE FATS

A sample of food can be tested for fats by shaking it in **ethanol**, which is a type of alcohol. Any fats **dissolve** in the ethanol. This **solution** can then be poured into water. Fats are **insoluble** in water, so tiny droplets of fat will form in water if they are present. A simpler test of fats is to press a sample of food between two sheets of paper. Fats and oils will leave a greasy mark on the paper.

Other fatty acids are missing more than one pair of hydrogen atoms. They are called polyunsaturates. ("Poly" means "many.") They are found in vegetable oils like sunflower oil.

Saturated fats, such as butter and lard, have a melting temperature of at least 20°C (68°F), so they are solid at room temperature. Monounsaturated fats, such as olive oil, are liquid at room temperature but turn cloudy and begin to thicken when they are kept in cold temperatures. Polyunsaturated fats, such as sunflower oil, always remain liquid, no matter how cold the temperature.

Fats can be solid or liquid, depending on the type of fatty acids they contain.

How Do We Get Fats from Food?

When you eat foods containing fats, your body needs to break the fats down so it can use them for energy and other body needs. Fats are broken down by your **digestive system**.

Eating and digesting

First you chew food, mashing it up and mixing it with **saliva** so it is softer and easier to swallow. Then the food passes down the esophagus into your stomach, where stomach acids and **enzymes** start to break it down. Enzymes are a type of protein. Their job is to speed up **chemical reactions** in cells.

Your stomach begins to digest proteins from your food, then passes it on to your **small intestine**. The small intestine's job is to break food down into **soluble** particles that can be absorbed into your blood.

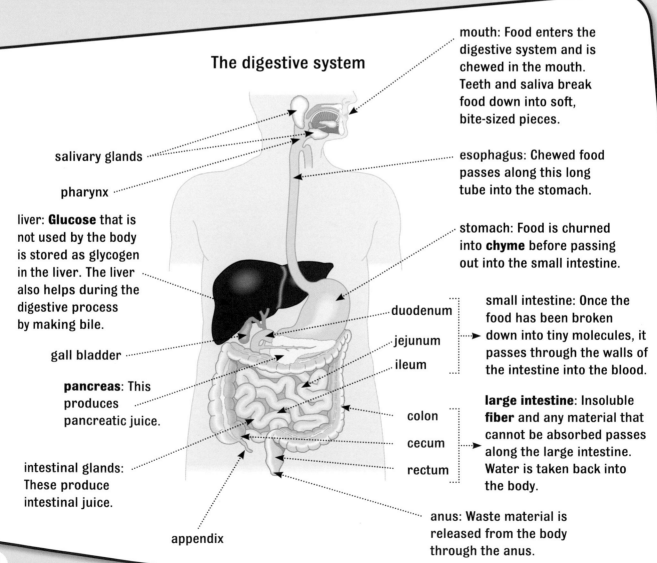

The digestive system

salivary glands

pharynx

liver: **Glucose** that is not used by the body is stored as glycogen in the liver. The liver also helps during the digestive process by making bile.

gall bladder

pancreas: This produces pancreatic juice.

intestinal glands: These produce intestinal juice.

appendix

mouth: Food enters the digestive system and is chewed in the mouth. Teeth and saliva break food down into soft, bite-sized pieces.

esophagus: Chewed food passes along this long tube into the stomach.

stomach: Food is churned into **chyme** before passing out into the small intestine.

duodenum

jejunum

ileum

small intestine: Once the food has been broken down into tiny molecules, it passes through the walls of the intestine into the blood.

large intestine: Insoluble **fiber** and any material that cannot be absorbed passes along the large intestine. Water is taken back into the body.

colon

cecum

rectum

anus: Waste material is released from the body through the anus.

Fats first have to be broken down so that they are small enough to be absorbed. Fats are insoluble in water, so a substance called **bile** does the job of breaking up fats from foods so that they can dissolve in water. Bile is made by the liver and stored in the gall bladder. After a meal, bile is released and passes into the small intestine, where it begins breaking up the fats you have just eaten. This process is called **emulsification**, and bile mixes with the fat, breaking up the large fat droplets into smaller droplets. This makes it easier for your body to absorb it.

EMULSIFICATION

You can watch emulsification happening to fats by pouring water into a greasy pan. A layer of fat will rise to the top of the water. If you add a few drops of liquid dish detergent, the fat will begin to emulsify and break down into smaller droplets.

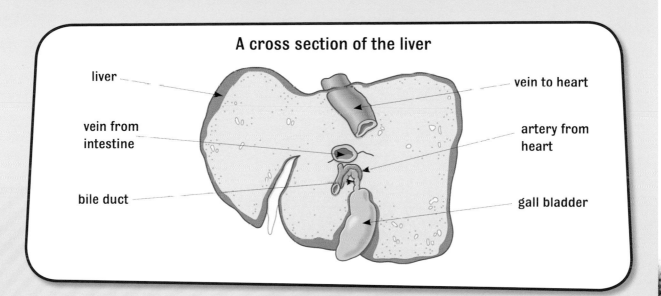

A cross section of the liver

liver

vein to heart

vein from intestine

artery from heart

bile duct

gall bladder

Fat stores facts

Your body can absorb and store fat in its liver, muscle, and fat cells. Fat cells make up fat tissue, which is found under the skin and cushioning internal organs such as the liver and kidneys. In liver and muscle cells, fat is stored as microscopic (so tiny you need a microscope to see them) droplets of fat. You can see these tiny droplets of fat in an animal's muscles as white streaks on meat.

How Does the Body Absorb Fats?

Absorbing fats

Once the bile has emulsified (broken down) the fats, your body needs to absorb them. Your pancreas sends out enzymes that attack the fat molecules. They break them down into fatty acids and **glycerol**. These are substances that can be absorbed into the cells that line your intestines.

Inside the cells of the small intestine, the fatty acids and glycerol are rebuilt into bundles of fat molecules called **triglycerides**. These fatty molecules have a protein coating that makes the fat dissolve more easily in water. They are now able to pass into your **lymphatic system**. Your lymphatic system uses liquids to carry substances around your body and get rid of waste matter and **toxins**. From the lymphatic system, fats can pass into your hepatic portal vein to the liver, and then into your bloodstream.

Your body now needs to absorb the fats being carried in your bloodstream into the fat, muscle, and liver cells. It can then either use the fats or store them as energy. It uses enzymes to break them down into fatty acids again. These enzymes are triggered by a hormone (chemical) called **insulin**.

ALL OF YOUR BODY NEEDS FAT FOR ENERGY

Your body needs to move fat to different parts, either to be used as energy or to be stored for later use. The fat molecules need to be broken into fatty acids because these smaller particles (tiny bits) can move between cells across the cell wall. However, when the body needs to transport fat around the body in the blood or in the lymph system, fatty acids are not the most efficient way. Lots of fatty acids attract lots of water, which would take up more energy, but fewer large fat molecules attract less water and use up less energy.

What is insulin?

Insulin is a hormone made in the body by the pancreas. It does an important job in helping your body build its energy stores. When you eat a meal or sweet snack, your body detects fatty acids, **amino acids**, and glucose in your intestine. Your brain tells your pancreas to produce insulin. Insulin works on many cells in the body, especially your liver, muscles, and fat cells. It encourages them to absorb fatty acids, glucose, and amino acids and to start using them to build your body's energy stores.

If levels of insulin in the body are high, the enzymes are very active. If levels of insulin are low, they are not active. The enzymes break down the fats in your blood into fatty acids and glycerol, which can be absorbed and stored in your liver, muscle, and fat cells. Inside these cells, insulin encourages the cells to form molecules of fat. These fat molecules are an important part of your body's energy stores.

Sometimes the body does not make enough insulin. This is called **diabetes**. People with diabetes can inject the insulin they need.

The intestinal lining

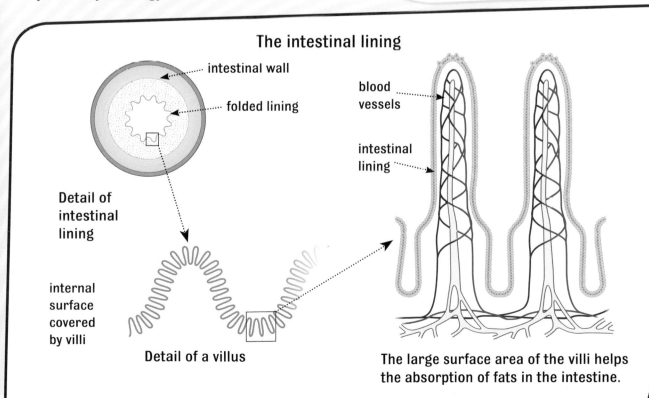

intestinal wall

folded lining

blood vessels

intestinal lining

Detail of intestinal lining

internal surface covered by villi

Detail of a villus

The large surface area of the villi helps the absorption of fats in the intestine.

How Does the Body Store Fat?

Fat is stored in tissue called adipose tissue. It is made up of fat cells. Fat cells are like tiny plastic bags that hold a droplet of fat inside. There are two types of fat cells: white fat and brown fat. White fat cells are large cells. They contain one large fat droplet. Brown fat cells are smaller. They contain several smaller fat droplets.

White fat is important for giving your body warmth, energy, and protective cushioning. Brown fat is found mainly in newborn babies, between their shoulders, and is important for keeping them warm.

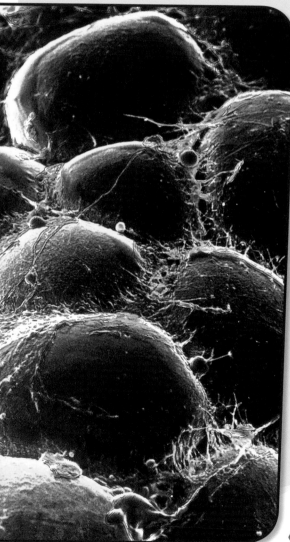

Babies and brown fat

Fat cells form in an unborn baby in the last three months of pregnancy. Newborn babies do not have much white fat stored, so they make warmth by breaking down the fat molecules in brown fat cells. Once babies start to eat more and grow, white fat begins to be stored in their white fat cells and replaces the brown fat. Adults have few or no brown fat cells. After **puberty**, the body makes no more fat cells. As it stores more fat, the number of fat cells remains the same, but the cells get bigger.

Some body fat is stored under your skin. It is important for keeping you warm because it does not allow heat to pass through it very easily. Fat also cushions and protects your internal organs, such as your kidneys.

Your body's fat cells are much less active than other cells. They do not **metabolize** fat; they just store it. When you eat a meal containing fats, your fat cells pick up spare fat in your bloodstream and store it.

 The fat cells that make up adipose tissue are some of the largest cells in the body.

Fat has a lot of energy per gram. Fat provides 9 calories per gram, whereas protein provides 4 calories, carbohydrate provides 4 calories, and alcohol provides 7 calories. If we consume more energy than we use up, the excess energy is stored as fat. This is why eating too many fatty foods, which provides lots of energy, may lead to weight gain.

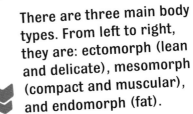

There are three main body types. From left to right, they are: ectomorph (lean and delicate), mesomorph (compact and muscular), and endomorph (fat).

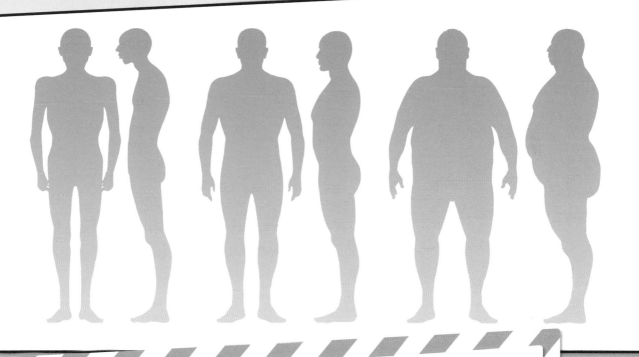

Body Mass Index

The Body Mass Index (BMI) can be calculated as follows:

$$\frac{\text{weight in pounds}}{(\text{height in inches})^2} \times 703$$

BMI	Weight status
under 18.5	underweight
18.5–24.9	healthy
25–29.9	overweight
over 30	obese

The BMI is used to find out whether a person's weight is appropriate for his or her height. Many factors, such as playing sports and family history, can have an effect on the BMI. It should not be used as the only measure of whether someone is overweight or obese.

How Does the Body Get Energy from Fats?

Your body gets energy from the food you eat. It can get energy from foods containing fats, carbohydrates, and proteins. For a healthy diet, you need to take energy from different food sources. Fats are the richest source of energy. They provide twice as much energy per gram as carbohydrates or proteins do. We measure the energy we take from food in calories (or kilojoules).

COMPARE THE ENERGY

- 1 gram of fat provides 9 calories of energy.
- 1 gram of carbohydrate provides 4 calories of energy.
- 1 gram of protein provides 4 calories of energy.

Why do you need energy?

Your body needs energy just to keep warm. You need energy for basic body processes like breathing, digesting food, and even sleeping. Young people need extra energy for growing. Your body is using energy even when you are resting. It uses energy to grow new cells and repair damaged cells.

The amount of energy you are using each minute when you are resting is called your **basal metabolic rate (BMR)**. An adult uses around 1.1 calories of energy for basic body processes each minute. Men have higher BMRs than women because they have more muscle to work. Older people tend to have lower BMRs because they have lost some of their muscle with aging. Infants and young children have a high BMR because they are using energy to grow. The basal metabolic rate accounts for about three-quarters of our total energy needs. The rest of our energy needs depend on our body weight and how active we are.

 When we are active, our bodies burn fat like cars burn fuel.

You need to take in enough energy from your food to stay a healthy weight for your size and give you energy for activities. You could run all day just on chocolate bars, but although they would give you energy, they would not provide the other nutrients you need from your diet. In **developed countries**, fats provide around 40 percent of the energy we take from our food. But health experts recommend that fats should provide no more than 35 percent of our total energy intake—around 78 grams (2.8 ounces) of fat if 2,000 calories are consumed. We should take about 50 percent of our energy from starchy carbohydrates, and the rest from proteins.

HOW MUCH DO YOU NEED?

The energy you need depends on your age and how active you are. A baby boy just under a year old needs about 920 calories of energy a day. A baby girl needs about 865 calories of energy a day. By the time they are between 11 and 14 years old, the boy needs about 2,220 calories of energy a day and the girl needs about 1,845 calories of energy a day.

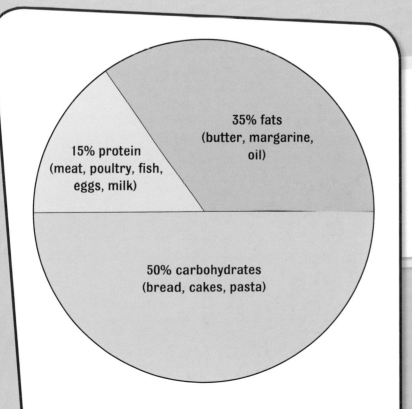

15% protein
(meat, poultry, fish, eggs, milk)

35% fats
(butter, margarine, oil)

50% carbohydrates
(bread, cakes, pasta)

The chart shows the percentages of total energy intake that should come from fats, carbohydrates, and proteins.

How Does the Body Turn Fats into Energy?

The more active you are, the more energy your body needs. When you are resting, your body is using just about one calorie each minute. Between meals, it can use fatty acids from your bloodstream as well as glucose to give you energy. When you start to become active, you will need more energy.

Where does the energy come from?

As you become more active, your body begins to take energy from glucose (blood sugar) in your blood. Glucose is the body's main source of energy. Some cells in your body, like your brain cells, can only get energy from glucose. Glucose is made from carbohydrate foods that you eat and then store in your liver as **glycogen**.

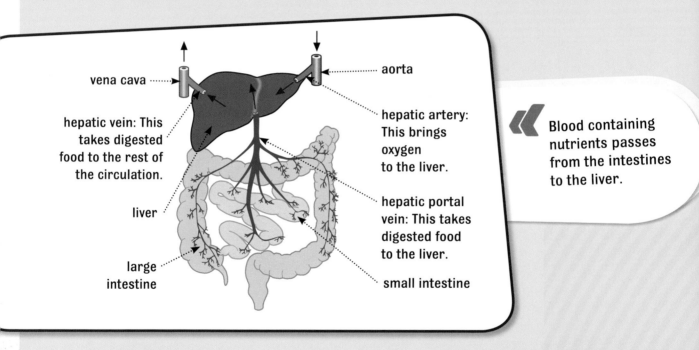

vena cava

hepatic vein: This takes digested food to the rest of the circulation.

liver

large intestine

aorta

hepatic artery: This brings oxygen to the liver.

hepatic portal vein: This takes digested food to the liver.

small intestine

Blood containing nutrients passes from the intestines to the liver.

The hepatic portal vein carries blood containing food nutrients from the intestine to the liver. The liver sorts through the blood. It removes chemical waste and stores useful substances like glucose and vitamins.

Energy for exercise

As you exercise, your body draws on stored carbohydrates and fats to give you energy. It first takes energy from muscle glycogen, which it has stored from starchy carbohydrate foods. The body can only store a certain amount of glycogen. The bigger your muscles are, the more glycogen they can hold.

When you are resting or performing light activities such as walking or writing, your body mainly metabolizes fat as a source of energy for your muscles. When you start to exercise, the working muscles need a more immediate source of energy, so the body switches from using fat to stored glycogen as the source of energy. Once all the glycogen has been used up, you start to feel tired and are forced to slow down as the muscles can only use fat for energy.

Trained athletes' bodies burn fat more quickly than normal people's bodies. The longer and harder they exercise, the more fat is burned for energy. After an hour of hard exercise, up to 75 percent of their energy may be provided by fats.

HOW MUCH ENERGY?

An adult uses an average of 2,400 calories of energy each day, depending on how active he or she is. A young man will use around 1.4 calories of energy each minute just sitting down. Walking slowly, he will use around 3 calories of energy each minute. If he plays soccer, the energy he uses will increase to 7 calories each minute.

Athletes who compete all over the world use a lot of energy every day.

Fats for Vitamins

You need some fats in your diet because they provide you with the vitamins A, D, E, and K, which you need to stay healthy. All these vitamins are **fat-soluble**, which means they are dissolved in the fats in your food. They are found in foods such as meat, liver, dairy foods, and leafy green vegetables. Some foods, such as milk and margarine, have vitamins A and D added to them. If you ate a very low fat diet for a long time, your body might not get enough of these important vitamins. When you digest foods containing fats, fat-soluble vitamins are carried into the intestine, where your body can absorb them.

Vitamin A

Vitamin A is found in oily fish, fish liver oils, liver, eggs, dairy products, and some vegetables, such as carrots. Your body needs it for growth, healthy skin, and good eyesight. A deficiency (shortage) of vitamin A can result in problems with eyesight and even blindness. Your body can only absorb vitamin A by taking it from fats in foods that you eat. You can get vitamin A from animal or vegetable foods. Animal sources of vitamin A are six times stronger than vegetable sources and can be toxic if you have too much.

The sunshine vitamin

Vitamin D is sometimes called the sunshine vitamin because sunlight is one source of it for your body. It is also found in liver, fish liver oils, oily fish, margarine, and fortified breakfast cereals. Vitamin D is important for forming healthy bones, and a deficiency of vitamin D can result in bone problems such as rickets.

Vitamin deficiency fact

The World Health Organization estimates that about 250 million children in **developing countries** suffer from vitamin A deficiency. It is a problem in 118 countries, especially in Africa and Southeast Asia. It can cause blindness and result in death and disease from infections, especially for children and pregnant women. The World Health Organization runs programs to give liquid vitamin A to children while they are being immunized (protected) against other diseases, such as polio.

Vitamin E

You need vitamin E for healthy skin, and it is also important for long-term health. It is found in eggs, liver, butter, milk, nuts, vegetable oils, and seeds.

Vitamin K

Vitamin K is important for healthy blood and circulation. It is found in green vegetables, tomatoes, eggs, and some cereals.

Vitamin stores

Your body can store fat-soluble vitamins in your liver and in your fat cells, until it needs them. You can fill up your vitamin stores by eating more of the right types of food. Some groups of people, like pregnant women, growing children, and the elderly, may need extra vitamins, but it is important not to take in too many fat-soluble vitamins, because they can build up in the liver and have toxic effects.

 These foods are part of a healthy diet because they contain **essential fatty acids** and vitamins.

Essential Fatty Acids

Your body can convert fatty acids from foods into different types of fatty acids to be used in different cells as it needs them. However, there are two types of **polyunsaturated fatty acids** (**PUFAs**) that your body cannot make, but that are essential for your health. These are called essential fatty acids (EFAs), and you can only get them by eating foods that contain them. The first is linoleic acid, found in vegetable seed oils such as sunflower oil, soybean oil, and in small amounts in animal fats, such as fatty meat. The second EFA is linolenic acid, found in small amounts in vegetable oils.

Polyunsaturated fatty acids (PUFAs)

Scientists group PUFAs into two families: **Omega 3 fatty acids** and **Omega 6 fatty acids**. They tell these fatty acids apart by looking at the chain of carbon and hydrogen atoms and finding out at which position along the chain the first missing hydrogen atom occurs. If the first missing hydrogen occurs at carbon atom number 3, the PUFA belongs to the Omega 3 family; if the first missing hydrogen occurs at carbon atom number 6, the PUFA belongs to the Omega 6 family.

 Foods like oily fish, nuts, and leafy green vegetables are all sources of fat-soluble vitamins.

Polyunsaturated fatty acids are found in fresh foods such as oily fish, green leafy vegetables, seeds and nuts, beans, and grains. The Omega 6 group are found in vegetable oils such as sunflower oil and margarines. The Omega 3 group are found in soybeans, walnuts, linseed and flax oil, dark green leafy vegetables, and oily fish such as tuna and mackerel. Linoleic acid belongs to the Omega 6 family, and linolenic acid belongs to the Omega 3 family of PUFAs.

Why do you need EFAs?

Many types of body cells, including your brain, nerve, skin, and hair cells, need EFAs to keep them healthy. They are also needed to help your body make hormones. EFAs are also important for the body's **immune system**, which defends the body against infections by **bacteria** and **viruses**.

How much fat do we need in our diets?

Current recommendations for fatty acid intake are that, on average, total fat and saturates should provide not more than 35 percent and 11 percent, respectively, of dietary energy intake. Monounsaturates should provide 13 percent of dietary energy. Polyunsaturates should provide 6.5 percent of energy, and a daily intake of 0.2 grams of Omega 3 polyunsaturates is also recommended. The essential fatty acids, linoleic acid and alpha linoleic acid, should provide at least 1 percent and 0.2 percent, respectively, of dietary energy.

Although not essential, other Omega 3 fatty acids may help protect you against heart disease by keeping your blood flowing smoothly and may also keep your joints healthy and protect you against diseases like arthritis.

STORING FATTY ACIDS

Fatty acids react easily with chemicals in the body, which is why they have health-giving powers. But this also means they can make foods containing them change chemically, so nuts and seeds can spoil or become stale when the fats in them **oxidize** (react with oxygen in the air). They need to be kept cool and stored in an airtight container.

Fats in Processed Foods

Foods like seeds and grains contain natural fatty acids. When we eat them, we also take in **fiber**, which the body needs to help keep the bowel healthy, and **antioxidant** vitamins, which it needs to keep cells healthy.

However, some fatty acids are chemically changed when food is processed. Fats are used in many processed foods, such as cooking oils and spreads, cakes, and ready-made meals. Manufacturers process natural foods to get the look and taste they want. They heat the food and use chemicals called **additives** to change the color, texture, taste, and smell.

Hydrogenated fats

One of these processes is called **hydrogenation**. It is used to turn **unsaturated** fats, which are liquid at room temperature, into a solid form for margarines, spreads, and cooking fats. It also makes fats less likely to spoil while foods are being stored. Hydrogenated fats are used to make crisp French fries and tasty doughnuts.

These fats can appear on food labels as "hydrogenated fat," "partially hydrogenated fat," "hardened fat," "vegetable fat," or "margarine." Hydrogenated fats may also be used for frying foods like fries.

Hydrogenation means adding hydrogen into fatty acid chains so they become "saturated" with hydrogen. Hydrogenation changes some of the unsaturated fats into saturated fats. The rest become **trans fats**. Trans fats help fats pack closely together so they stay solid at room temperature, like a margarine spread.

Pastries are often made using hydrogenated fat.

Trans fats

Natural trans fats are sometimes found in small amounts in foods such as meat and dairy foods. However, most trans fats come from fried foods and high-fat processed foods such as margarines, spreads, doughnuts, cakes, and crackers.

A high level of trans fats in the diet has undesirable effects on blood **cholesterol** levels, by causing an increase in **LDL cholesterol** levels and a decrease in **HDL cholesterol** levels. This can increase the risk of heart disease. Keeping your consumption under 5 grams per day is best for your health, but your goal should be 0 grams a day. This target has been helped by many manufacturers removing trans fats from their products.

FRYING FAT

Fats can also change chemically when they are heated at high temperatures. Frying can make some cooking oils oxidize (react with oxygen) and create chemicals called **free radicals**, which can damage and age body cells. Butter and olive oil are less likely to oxidize at high temperatures.

 Fats can change chemically when they are heated at high temperatures.

Fat and Cholesterol

Cholesterol is a type of fat found in your body. Your body needs some cholesterol to build cell walls and brain and nerve tissue. It also uses cholesterol to make hormones needed for basic processes like digestion. Your body can make about 75 percent of the cholesterol it needs from the dietary fat that you eat. One of the things cholesterol is used for is to be converted into bile acids, which help digest and absorb fat from the diet.

Dietary cholesterol

You also take in some cholesterol from your diet. Dietary cholesterol is found in animal foods, such as egg yolks, meat, liver, some shellfish, and milk. Unless you have a very high intake, dietary cholesterol has little effect on cholesterol levels in your blood. Blood cholesterol levels are mainly affected by intake of saturates.

Blood cholesterol levels

Good cholesterol molecules (called HDL cholesterol) help carry cholesterol and fats away from the **arteries** to the liver, where they can be safely broken down. HDL cholesterol can help protect the body against heart disease. But bad cholesterol molecules (called LDL cholesterol) can slowly build up in the walls of the arteries that feed blood to the heart and brain. This can start to form fatty deposits that clog the arteries. If a **blood clot** forms, it can block the flow of blood and oxygen to the heart muscle and cause a heart attack. It if blocks the flow of blood and oxygen to the brain, it can cause a **stroke**.

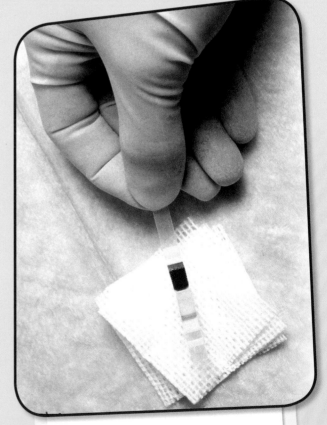

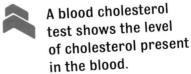 A blood cholesterol test shows the level of cholesterol present in the blood.

Controlling cholesterol

Doctors measure the amount of cholesterol in the blood in millimoles per liter of blood (mmol/l). They recommend that blood cholesterol should be below 5.0 mmol/l in order to help prevent heart disease. Diets in countries such as the United States, which are high in animal foods, can often lead to high blood cholesterol. Doctors recommend reducing blood cholesterol by making changes in diet and lifestyle.

Lowering cholesterol

Blood cholesterol levels can be lowered by reducing the intake of saturates from the diet. Replacing saturates with monounsaturates and polyunsaturates can help lower LDL cholesterol and raise or maintain HDL cholesterol levels. Other foods such as oatmeal, which contain soluble fiber, may also help reduce blood cholesterol levels. There are also some food products, such as yogurts and margarine spreads, that can help lower blood cholesterol. They contain a plant ingredient called plant stanol ester, which stops the body from absorbing dietary cholesterol.

 Low fat foods can help control the amount of dietary cholesterol. Some foods can even help reduce cholesterol in the body.

CONTROL CHOLESTEROL BY:

- losing excess weight
- getting more exercise
- avoiding too many foods high in saturates
- eating a low fat diet
- eating foods that contain fiber, such as fruits, vegetables, whole grains, and cereals.

Fats and Overeating

When you take in more energy than you use up, the excess energy is stored as fat and can lead you to become overweight. Foods containing a lot of fat provide more energy than those that contain mainly either carbohydrate or protein. People like high fat foods such as burgers, fries, cakes, and doughnuts because their fat content gives them a nice taste and "mouth-feel"; this is what can tempt people to overeat.

Obesity

A recent survey of adults in the United States showed that 67 percent of men and 62 percent of women were overweight, and 28 percent of men and 34 percent of women were obese. A person who is obese has a much greater risk of developing diseases such as diabetes, heart disease, high blood pressure, and some cancers. Therefore, these people should be encouraged to lose weight. Weight may be lost by decreasing energy intake and increasing physical activity. The best way to decrease energy intake is to avoid eating too many energy-dense foods, which tend to be high in fat.

Scientists are studying the effects of how a "fat gene" may cause obesity.

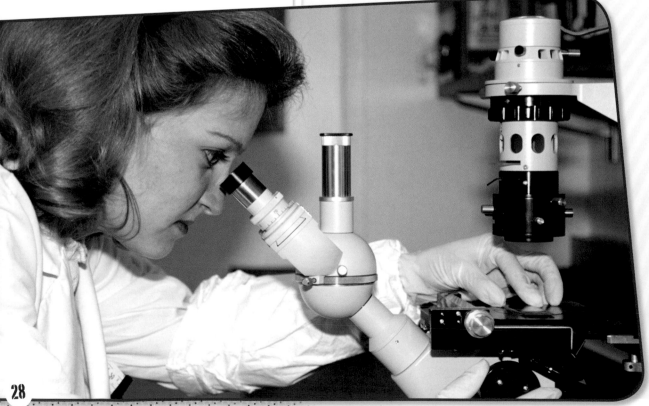

Fat and the basal metabolic rate

Fat cells are not as active as other body cells. They use a lot less energy than muscle cells, for example. The more fat and less muscle the body carries, the lower the basal metabolic rate (see page 16) of that person will be.

When people want to lose weight, they should reduce their energy intake and become more active so that they use up more energy than they take in. People wanting to lose weight should not reduce their energy intake by too much, or they will start to lose muscle as well as fat. It is important that people who are dieting get a good intake of all the essential nutrients. This means that the diet should be high in fruits and vegetables and include high fiber, low fat foods.

People can increase both their basal metabolic rate and their overall **metabolic rate** through exercise and physical activity. Exercises that develop muscle, such as weight training or jobs that involve lifting and carrying, mean that the body will be using up more energy even when resting. Activities such as running, dancing, and playing sports are called **cardiovascular** exercise and use up a lot of energy while you are doing them. Running for 30 minutes can use up to 300 calories. This is why experts recommend a combination of exercises and activities for weight loss.

 Obesity is a growing problem in many parts of the developed world.

Fats and Obesity

We need to eat just enough fats to keep our body healthy and to give us energy. If we are active and get lots of exercise, our body will use the fats we eat to give it energy. By balancing our energy intake and output, we will stay a healthy weight.

FAT RATS!

In a study at the University of Illinois, one group of rats was fed a diet of 42 percent fats (the average fat intake for people in developed countries). The other group was fed on a low fat diet. After 60 weeks, the low fat group was still lean and sleek. The high fat group was overweight and had up to 51 percent body fat.

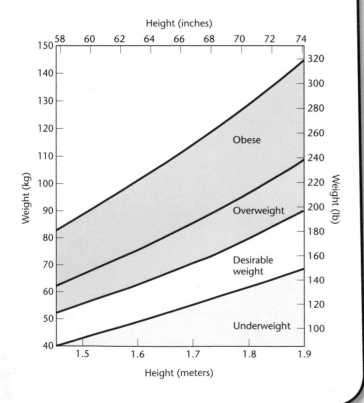

Height/weight chart

Fat lifestyles

It is normal to store fat in infancy and adolescence. But the diet and lifestyle we have today mean that many children and adults are overweight. Popular foods such as burgers and fries, pastries, and ice cream are high in fat. Many processed foods carry hidden fats. Also, people get much less exercise than they used to. People used to walk and cycle to work and school. Now many people go by car or public transportation. In the past, people were more active in their leisure time, too. Now they spend more time watching television or using computers. Even central heating stops us from using energy to keep ourselves warm. Sitting in a warm room watching television uses as little energy as sleeping!

Obesity

More and more people are becoming obese. People are classified as obese when they have a BMI of 30 or above. In the United States, one in three adults is obese. About 30 percent of U.S. schoolchildren are overweight; about 15 percent are obese. Childhood obesity in the United States has more than tripled in the past two decades. Obese kids are likely to grow into obese adults. The main causes of obesity are poor diet and lack of exercise.

Scientists are researching drugs to fight obesity, but the best way of tackling it is to reduce the amount of calories eaten each day, eat a low fat diet, and get more exercise.

Exercise fact

Regular exercise helps burn off fat stores, and it may also speed up the metabolic rate—the rate at which the body turns food into energy—by up to 10 times.

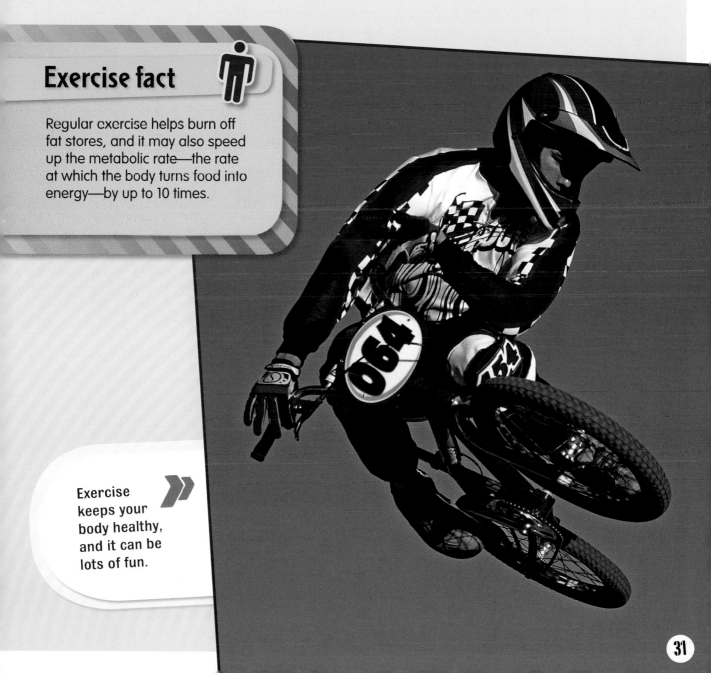

Exercise keeps your body healthy, and it can be lots of fun.

Fats and Health Problems

Fats should make up no more than 35 percent of your diet. This will give you plenty of energy and all your essential fatty acids. However, in developed countries such as the United States, the diet, which contains lots of fatty products, can take approximately 40 percent of total energy intake from fats.

Health problems

A high fat diet can cause many health problems. Some of these are linked with obesity. Obesity increases the risk of coronary heart disease, stroke, diabetes and some cancers. Doctors believe that an "apple" body shape, which carries most fat around the middle, is more at risk from health problems than a "pear" shape, which carries most weight around the hips and thighs.

Obesity puts extra stress on many parts of the body, such as the bones, blood circulation, and nerves. It increases the risk of osteoarthritis, where the joints become painful and swollen. It also increases the risk of diabetes, which means the body does not produce enough insulin or use it properly. Obesity can also lead to high blood pressure, heart and breathing problems, and some types of cancer.

>> Saturated fats are found in:
- meat and dairy food
- some plant oils, such as coconut and palm oil
- processed foods such as cakes, cookies, and chips.

French fries might be tasty, but if you eat them too often you will run the risk of damaging your health. >>

Cancer

Diets that are high in fat, especially saturates, have been directly linked with some cancers, including cancer of the breast, colon, and skin.

Doctors believe about 30 to 40 percent of all cancers could be prevented by eating a diet that is low in fat and high in fiber and by getting regular exercise. They recommend diets that are low in fat and high in plant foods, such as fresh fruits and vegetables, to prevent cancer. You should aim to eat at least five portions of a variety of fruits and vegetables every day. This includes canned, frozen, and dried types, as well as fresh.

You can reduce your intake of saturates by choosing lean meat and removing visible fat or skin on meat where possible, and by choosing low fat dairy products such as skimmed milk and reduced fat cheese. You can also avoid eating too many fatty meat products, cakes, cookies, and pastries.

Cancer fact

Women in Japan have low rates of breast cancer compared to women who live in western countries. They eat a diet that is low in saturates and high in fish oils and soy protein. When Japanese women move to a western country and eat a western diet, their rate of breast cancer increases.

Sushi—often made with raw fish—is a popular part of the Japanese diet.

Fats and Heart Disease

Eating too many saturates in the diet increases the risk of heart disease. Heart disease causes about 40 percent of all deaths in the United States!

Blocking arteries

Having a high intake of saturates in the diet raises the level of cholesterol in the blood. The cholesterol can accumulate in the walls of the vessels in the heart. Once it starts to build up, it can oxidize and cause the vessels to become clogged and narrow as the overgrowth in the vessel walls becomes a hardened plaque. This leads to a reduced flow of blood to the heart and may cause chest pain (angina), particularly during exercise.

As the fats and cholesterol begin to build up, they gather calcium, which causes the artery walls to begin to harden. This thickening and hardening of the artery walls is called arteriosclerosis. It can be caused by:

- eating too many saturates
- having high levels of blood cholesterol
- smoking
- not getting enough exercise
- being obese
- having high blood pressure
- having diabetes.

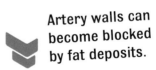

Artery walls can become blocked by fat deposits.

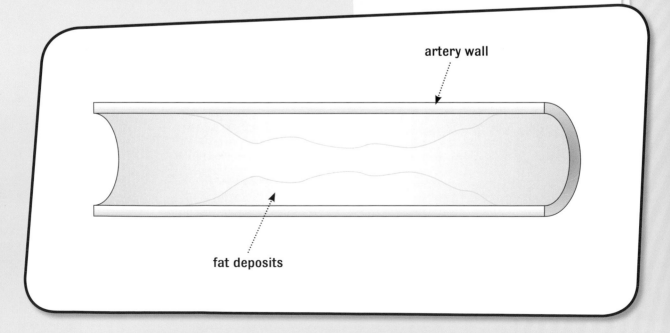

artery wall

fat deposits

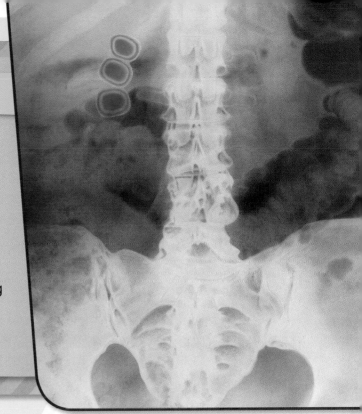

Gallstone fact

The gallbladder is like a small bag just below your liver. It makes green liquid called bile to help you break down fats and other substances in your food. Sometimes hard stones called gallstones are produced. They may go unnoticed, but at other times they can become very painful and need surgery to fix. Factors such as family history, age, and gender can affect the likelihood of a person getting gallstones. However, it is thought that eating more fruits and vegetables and less fat can help to prevent them.

Angina and heart attack

As the arteries get thicker and harder, it is more difficult for blood to flow around the body. When someone starts to exercise, his or her heart has to work harder to try to pump blood to the muscles.

 Gallstones form in the gall bladder.

The person can start to get pains in the legs because the muscles are not getting enough blood and oxygen. He or she can also get pain around the heart muscle if it is not getting enough blood and oxygen. This heart pain is called angina.

Eventually, the thick, sticky blood can form a blood clot, which blocks an artery. If it blocks an artery that leads to the heart, it can cause a heart attack. If it blocks an artery leading to the brain, it can cause a stroke.

DON'S STORY

Don Salmon was in his early sixties and had just retired from his job as a truck driver when he suffered a heart attack. Don used to be a smoker and enjoyed a breakfast of bacon and eggs every day. Doctors found he had a high blood cholesterol level. They recommended that he cut out red meat, eat no more than three eggs a week, and use low fat dairy products. This has helped Don reduce the risk of another heart attack.

Fats Preventing Disease

A high intake of saturates and trans fats can both raise blood cholesterol levels and lead to heart disease. However, some unsaturates may help protect against heart disease by lowering bad cholesterol and raising or maintaining good cholesterol in the blood.

Healthy fats

Monounsaturates, such as olive oil, and polyunsaturates, such as sunflower oil, may lower blood cholesterol levels. They also provide vitamin E, which may protect against heart disease. Nuts, especially walnuts and almonds, are also rich in polyunsaturated fatty acids, which can protect against heart disease and lower blood cholesterol. Monounsaturates may also increase levels of the good HDL cholesterol, and so help protect against heart disease.

HEALTHY EATING

Mediterranean countries, such as Greece, Italy, and Spain, have 50 to 70 percent less heart disease than the United States. Southern Europeans eat mainly unsaturates in their diet. Red meat is only eaten a few times a month, on special occasions. Small amounts of fish, poultry, and eggs are also eaten. They eat lots of starchy carbohydrates, such as bread, pasta, and potatoes, and plenty of fresh fruits and vegetables. They cook with olive oil, which is high in monounsaturates.

 Patients recovering from a heart attack are advised to eat a healthier diet.

Diets across the world

The diet typically eaten in the United States contains high levels of saturates, from meat and dairy foods, and also from cooking by roasting or frying. In other parts of the world, meat is only used to add flavor and texture to a meal or is saved for special occasions. Cooking is based on starchy carbohydrates, such as rice and couscous, eaten with pulses (peas, beans, and lentils) and vegetables. Low levels of saturated fats are linked with lower rates of heart disease.

Fish is good for the heart

Omega 3 fatty acids, which are found in fish oils, may help improve blood flow to the heart. Eating oily fish, such as mackerel, salmon, or tuna, twice a week will provide around 1 gram a day of Omega 3 fatty acids. This may prevent blood clots from forming and protect against heart disease.

Diet fact

The Japanese diet contains just over 30 percent fat, compared with 40 percent in the United States. Japanese cooking is based on rice, fresh vegetables, and oily fish, which are all rich in polyunsaturated fatty acids. Japan has one of the lowest rates of heart disease in the world. The Inuit people of Greenland also have a low rate of heart disease. Their diet is based on fish and marine animals, which are low in saturated fat and high in Omega 3 fatty acids.

Asian diets are based on foods that are high in starchy carbohydrates and low in fat.

Getting Enough Fat

Eating too much fatty food is bad for your health, but not eating any fat would stop the body from getting important nutrients. We must eat some fat to get the essential fatty acids, which the body cannot make itself. Deficiency in these fatty acids can cause growth problems, arthritis, and other health problems.

Omega 6 fatty acids

We need Omega 6 fatty acids to build healthy cell walls and make hormones and chemicals that control body processes such as blood flow. Some people can have an Omega 6 deficiency because their bodies are not able to absorb fats properly. We need to eat about 2 grams of Omega 6 fatty acids a day.

We also need about 0.2 grams of Omega 3 fatty acids a day. Omega 3 fatty acids are needed when the body is growing in order to build healthy brain and eye tissue and to keep blood flowing properly.

Fat for vitamins

The body needs some fat each day to provide and absorb enough of the fat-soluble vitamins A, D, E, and K. When fats are removed from dairy products to make low fat products such as yogurts, skimmed milk, and cottage cheese, these foods lose much of their vitamin A content. The body can make extra vitamin A from beta-carotene, which is found in leafy green and orange vegetables and orange and yellow fruits. But it needs fats in the diet to be able to absorb beta-carotene and fat-soluble vitamins.

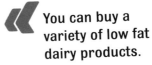
You can buy a variety of low fat dairy products.

VEGETARIANS AND VITAMIN A

In Africa, many people can only afford to eat meat on special occasions. If babies and young children do not get enough fats from plant foods, they can develop vitamin A deficiency, which can lead to blindness.

Fats and growth

Fats are needed to help babies grow properly, and also during puberty when the body is growing rapidly. A baby grows to three times its birth weight in its first year. Fat is a natural part of breast milk. It provides around half the total daily intake of calories until the baby is about one year old and starts eating solid foods.

Babies should not be fed cows' milk until after one year. They should have special formula milk or breast milk. Children under the age of two years should drink whole milk, after which semi-skimmed (2%) milk may be introduced. Skimmed milk is not suitable for children under five.

Babies need to drink full fat milk until they are about two years old. Solids, such as prepared baby foods, eventually take the place of the liquid diet.

Balancing Fats in the Diet

A healthy diet needs to be low in saturates and have a good balance of unsaturates, including Omega 6 and Omega 3 fatty acids. However, in western countries such as the United States, most of the fats in our diet are saturates from red meat, dairy products, and sweets.

Health recommendations

Health experts recommend that most people in the United States reduce the amount of saturates from animal foods in their diet and increase the amounts of unsaturates from fish and plant foods. Cholesterol in the diet tends to be found in foods that are high in saturates.

We can get a healthy balance of fats in our diet by:
* using butter and spreads sparingly
* drinking semi-skimmed (2%) or skimmed milk
* eating no more than three to four eggs a week
* eating less fatty meat and more oily fish
* cutting the fat off meat and skin off chicken
* avoiding too many fried foods, such as French fries
* using olive oil or sunflower oil for cooking rather than hard fats such as butter or lard
* avoiding too many processed foods that contain saturated or hydrogenated fats.

Fats on food labels

Read food labels to check the fat content. Food labels may list the total fat content per 100 grams (3.5 ounces), as well as the amount of saturates and unsaturates. They may also give the percentage of fat per serving. Look for low levels of saturates and higher levels of unsaturates.

Total fat—what's high and what's low?
High is more than 20 grams of fat per 100 grams.
Low is 3 grams of fat or less per 100 grams.
Saturated fat—what's high and what's low?
High is more than 5 grams of saturates per 100 grams.
Low is 1.5 grams of saturates or less per 100 grams.

Processed food

Seventy percent of the fat that we eat is hidden in processed foods. Try to avoid eating too many processed foods such as cakes, crackers, snack bars, and chips. Lots of products that contain hydrogenated fats have had the trans fats removed.

We can try to balance our intake of higher fat foods with low fat foods to keep our total fat intake to about 20 to 35 percent of total calories each day. Look for low fat food products such as semi-skimmed (2%) or skimmed milk, low fat yogurt, baked chips, or reduced fat cheese. But beware of labels claiming "90% fat free"—the product still contains 10 percent fat!

Low cholesterol foods

Some foods claim to lower blood cholesterol. They include fat and cheese spreads and yogurts. They contain plant substances called plant sterols or plant stanol ester.

 Stir-frying is a healthy way of cooking because it only uses small amounts of oil.

COOKING WITH FATS

Choose healthy ways of cooking such as grilling, steaming, and baking, rather than frying and roasting. Stir-frying uses less fat than deep frying. Hard fats such as lard and butter are high in saturates, so it is healthier to cook with vegetable oils such as olive oil or sunflower oil. Never reuse old cooking oil or eat burned foods, as they can contain the substances called free radicals, which can damage your health.

Fats in the Food Pyramid

The "MyPyramid" food pyramid divides foods into five food groups (plus oils and fats) and shows the types and proportions of foods that make a healthy diet.

GRAINS | VEGETABLES | FRUITS | MILK | MEAT & BEANS

Guidelines for eating well

1 Base your meals on starchy foods.
2 Eats lots of fruits and vegetables.
3 Eat more fish.
4 Cut down on saturated fat and sugar.
5 Try to eat less salt—no more than 6 grams a day.
6 Get active and try to be a healthy weight.
7 Drink plenty of water.
8 Don't skip breakfast.

Try to include a variety of red fruits (for example, red grapes and berries), orange fruits and vegetables (oranges, carrots), and green fruits and vegetables (peas, beans, green grapes, and so on) in your diet.

 Eating a variety of fruits allows you to get the widest range of nutrients.

Balance fats so that you eat mainly polyunsaturates or monounsaturates from foods such as oily fish, nuts, seeds, and vegetable oils. Keep foods that are high in saturates, such as fries, cakes, and chips, as occasional treats.

Get a healthy balance

Fats have an important role to play in a healthy diet. Some fats are better for us than others, and it is up to us to see that we get the balance right for our bodies.

Glossary

additive substance added to preserve or add flavor to food

amino acid part of food that makes up proteins and helps break them down when food is being digested

antioxidant type of vitamin or substance believed to protect body cells from damage and aging

artery blood vessel that carries blood from your heart to other parts of your body

atom smallest part of any chemical

bacteria tiny living organism; some are helpful in the body, but others can be harmful

basal metabolic rate (BMR) energy we use each minute for basic body processes

bile substance made in the liver that helps break down fats

blood clot thick mass of blood that can block arteries

calorie measurement of energy supplied by food

carbohydrate part of food that we need for energy

carbon simple chemical substance that is part of the makeup of fatty acids

cardiovascular having to do with the heart and the blood system

cell smallest unit of a plant or animal

chemical reaction when two or more chemicals react together to produce a change

cholesterol substance made by the body and found in some foods. It is necessary for certain functions of the body, but can lead to health problems if too much cholesterol is formed and deposited on the walls of blood vessels.

chyme mushy liquid that passes from the stomach to the small intestine. It is formed from partly digested food mixed with the digestive juices of the stomach.

developed country country (usually western) that has well-established industries and services, such as transportation, schools, and welfare

developing countries poorer countries that do not have well established industries and services, such as transport, schools, welfare

diabetes disease where the body cannot control the level of sugar in the blood

digestive system parts of the body that work to process food

dissolve break down in water

emulsification process of breaking down fat so it can dissolve in water

energy power to be physically and mentally active

enzyme chemical agent that changes food into substances we can absorb

essential fatty acid (EFA) fatty acid that the body needs but can only get from food

ethanol type of alcohol

fat-soluble can dissolve in fats

fatty acid molecule made from a chain of carbon and hydrogen atoms, with one oxygen atom attached

fiber part of food that we need for healthy digestion

free radical chemical substance that may harm health

gene information in the form of a body chemical, DNA, that carries the instructions for a living thing to develop and survive. These chemical instructions are inherited from parents.

germ (of wheat or corn) central part of grain that contains oil

glucose type of sugar made from carbohydrate and broken down in muscles to give energy

glycerol simple substance that is part of the makeup of fats

glycogen form in which glucose is stored in muscles

HDL cholesterol fatty substance carried in the blood by high density lipoproteins, which help reduce the risk of heart disease

hormone chemical made by cells in the body and carried by the blood

husk dry outer coating of a seed

hydrogen simple chemical substance that is part of the makeup of fatty acids

hydrogenation process used to make fats solid

immune system body's defenses against germs and diseases

insoluble cannot be dissolved in water

insulin type of hormone produced by the pancreas to control the amount of sugar in the blood

kilojoule unit of energy in food

large intestine part of the intestines through which undigested food passes after it has left the small intestine

LDL cholesterol fatty substance carried in the blood by "low density lipoproteins." A large amount circulating in the blood increases the risk of heart disease.

liver organ in the body used in the digestive system. It makes bile and helps clean the blood.

lymphatic system liquid system that carries substances around the body and clears away waste matter

metabolic rate speed at which your body's chemical reactions occur

metabolize to change or break down a substance into something the body needs such as energy

mineral nutrient found in foods that the body needs to stay healthy

molecule simple unit of a chemical substance

monounsaturated fatty acid that has one pair of hydrogen atoms missing

nutrient substance that the body needs to stay healthy

obese when a person's Body Mass Index (BMI) is 30 or above

Omega 3 fatty acids group of PUFAs that contain the EFA linolenic acid

Omega 6 fatty acids group of PUFAs that contain the EFA linoleic acid

organ part inside the body that has particular jobs to do

oxidize combine with oxygen to make an oxide

oxygen colorless gas needed for animals and plants to live

pancreas part of the body that makes insulin and enzymes to digest food

polyunsaturated fatty acid that has more than one pair of hydrogen atoms missing

polyunsaturated fatty acid (PUFA) fatty acid that the body either makes or has to get from food

protein part of food that people need for growth and energy

puberty time when a child's body matures so he or she is capable of having children

saliva fluid made by glands in the mouth, which are needed to digest food

saturated fatty acid that is saturated with hydrogen atoms

small intestine part of the intestine into which food passes from the stomach to be digested and then absorbed into the blood. Undigested food passes through the small intestine into the large intestine.

soluble can dissolve in water

solution liquid that has a substance dissolved in it

starch type of carbohydrate found in food such as bread that takes longer to digest than sugars

stroke sudden change in blood supply to the brain, which can cause loss of movement in parts of the body

tissue an organized group of cells in an organism, such as bone or cartilage

toxin poisonous substance

trans fat type of fat made by hydrogenation

triglyceride chemical form in which fats exist in foods and in the body

unsaturated fatty acid that is not saturated with hydrogen atoms

virus tiny living organism that can cause disease

vitamin nutrient found in food that we need to stay healthy

Find Out More

Books

Sheen, Barbara. *The Real Deal: Eating Right.* Chicago: Raintree, 2008.

Thomas, Isabel. *Real World Data: Graphing Food and Nutrition.* Chicago: Heinemann Library, 2009.

Watson, Stephanie. *Trans Fats.* New York: Rosen Central, 2008.

Websites

www.cnpp.usda.gov
This site from the Center for Nutrition Policy and Promotion, a part of the U.S. Department of Agriculture, provides information about health and nutrition. Included is the "MyPyramid" food pyramid, which offers guidelines for a healthy, balanced diet.

www.americanheart.org
Visit the website of the American Heart Association.

www.nutrition.gov
Learn more about nutrition at this educational site set up by the U.S. Department of Agriculture.

www.diabetes.org
Find out more information about diabetes.

Index